Walmer C
and Gardens

KENT

History by
J G COAD MA, FSA
Inspector of Ancient Monuments and Historic Buildings

Rooms and their Contents by
G E HUGHES BA
Regional Curator of Works of Art

Walmer Castle was built in 1539 as one of a chain of coastal artillery forts constructed by Henry VIII against the threat of invasion by Spain. From 1708 it became the official residence of the Lords Warden of the Cinque Ports, an historic title dating from the thirteenth century. The castle's martial appearance has been much modified by the alterations of successive Lords Warden in transforming the imposing fortress into a comfortable residence. The office of Lord Warden was originally created to regulate the powerful confederation of the five ports of Hastings, Romney, Hythe, Dover and Sandwich, whose citizens gained royal privileges in return for defending the ports, but in recent years the title has been conferred primarily as a distinguished honour.

ENGLISH HERITAGE · LONDON

fortresses were functional, purposeful structures, shorn of most adornments and normally garrisoned and armed fully only in times of war. Not merely on account of their cost, but also because of their power, the great majority of artillery fortresses in Europe were built and controlled by states, and not by private individuals.

Early Artillery Defences in England

Mainland Europe, with its numerous vulnerable land frontiers, had greater cause than England to develop and construct the new fortresses. In England, artillery had begun to be added to fortifications in the latter part of the fourteenth century.

After the death of Edward III in 1377 and the decline in England's military fortunes in the Hundred Years War (1337–1453), the Channel coast and its hinterland became vulnerable to frequent and destructive raids. As a direct consequence, gun-ports were added to the town defences of Canterbury and Southampton, while new castles were built at Cooling in Kent (1381) and Bodiam in Sussex (1385), among other places. In all these cases, the form and design of the fortifications remained essentially medieval – the high curtain walls and towers of Bodiam castle were identical in concept to the great Edwardian castles of Wales of a century earlier.

Only towards the very end of the fifteenth century and the beginning of the sixteenth is there evidence that military engineers in England were building artillery defences comparable with the more advanced designs common on mainland Europe. The still-surviving D-shaped earthwork at the frontier town of Berwick-upon-Tweed dates from then, as did the now-vanished bastioned defences around Portsmouth. All these English fortifications were piecemeal developments, the result of local initiatives by individuals or towns seeing themselves threatened by raids.

Henry VIII's Invasion Defences

Walmer Castle, begun in the spring of 1539, was designed to meet a far more serious threat. Henry VIII's break with the Roman Catholic Church and his destruction of the monasteries had infuriated the papacy and deeply offended the Catholic powers of Europe. One of these, the Emperor Charles V had personal cause for displeasure following Henry's divorce of the Emperor's aunt, Catherine of Aragon in 1533. All this had mattered little to Henry and to England while the two principal Catholic military powers of Europe, Spain and France, were openly hostile to each other. But in June 1538, a few months ahead of the papal Bull excommunicating Henry VIII, Francis I of France and the Emperor Charles V staged a reconciliation. On both sides of the Channel a crusade against the heretical English king was seen as a distinct possibility.

The reaction of Henry and his advisers was robust. Preparations to counter an invasion began in earnest early in 1539 at the same time as the final destruction of the greater religious houses was nearing its climax. Musters of able-bodied men were held, the small fleet was readied, the warning chain of beacons around the coast was refurbished and manned, while extra weapons and mercenaries were sought in Antwerp and Hamburg.

Most significantly, in February 1539 Henry ordered specially appointed commissioners to survey the coasts of England for sites for fortifications to protect likely invasion beaches, dockyards, fleet anchorages, ports and harbours. In practice this meant the southern half of the country nearest to France and the Low

Countries. The chain of defences from Hull to Milford Haven ultimately constructed as a result of this survey was the first system of coastal defences since the Roman forts of the Saxon Shore over 1200 years earlier. Like the Roman forts, this Tudor chain was conceived to broadly standard designs and was entirely financed by the state.

To be effective against a major invasion, Henry's defences had to be strong enough to withstand bombardment from hostile ships – not admittedly a serious threat given the then state of naval ordnance and warship design – and to withstand siege on the assumption that a hostile army and its heavy weapons had been able to effect a landing. The great majority of the new works were thus designed for all-round defence, although a number of simpler gun batteries were also constructed.

The Castles of the Downs

Walmer Castle, along with Deal and the now largely-vanished Sandown Castle, was sited to protect this low-lying coast and to dominate the Downs – a great stretch of water sheltered by the Goodwin Sands. The open roadstead of the Downs was a favourite anchorage for merchant shipping and naval vessels, a victualling station, as well as an embarkation point for the Continent. The Emperor Charles V himself had departed from here in 1520 after his visit to Henry VIII at Canterbury, while it was not unknown for hostile vessels to lie off hoping to prey on merchant shipping. In 1495 Perkin Warbeck's forces made their abortive landing at Deal. In the invasion scare of 1539, protection of this part of the coast was not surprisingly given priority.

The 1539 proposals led to the construction of the castles of Walmer, Deal and Sandown. In between were placed four earth bulwarks or gun batteries, and all seven fortifications appear to have been linked by a defensible trench or covered way extending for two-and-a-half miles. The trench, as might be expected, appears to have had a fairly short life, but the four bulwarks survived into the late eighteenth century, although apparently long disused.

Such was the perceived danger that, by May 1539, 1400 men were at work and more were being recruited. By December 1539 Deal Castle was sufficiently advanced to be the setting for a banquet to welcome Anne of Cleeves after her landing at the Downs on her way to her brief marriage to Henry VIII. By the following summer, the earth bulwarks and covered way had been completed and the last payment for works at the Downs appears in the royal accounts for early September 1540. By the following month all the defences here were garrisoned.

Since the completion of this remarkable concentration of Tudor defence works alongside the Downs, much has changed. Today the Downs roadstead, save when severe storms are forecast, is generally empty of shipping, a far cry from the days of sailing ships when it could be crowded with many dozens of vessels either sheltering, taking on victuals and passengers or merely awaiting favourable winds. The earthworks have totally vanished, while only a residual stub of the keep of Sandown remains in part of the sea defence works. Urban spread has now united the formerly separate communities of Walmer and Deal, and houses and trees obscure views along the coastal strip. But initially, and for some time after their completion, the defences here must have dominated the scene, the earth bulwarks overawed by the three great stone fortresses. Deal Castle is the largest of the three, with Walmer and Sandown near identical to each other in size and design.

Walmer Castle has all the characteristic features of the stone and brick fortresses

The 'Three Castles in the Downs', an early eighteenth-century oil-painting in the Dining Room

built by Henry VIII between 1539 and 1542. The heart of the castle is the central circular keep, surrounded by an open courtyard and protected by a concentric curtain wall. From the latter project four squat bastions, each slightly more than a semi-circle. The northern one incorporates a gateway approached across the moat by a bridge and drawbridge, while the moat itself has a stone-faced counterscarp or

outer wall. A gallery running round the castle at basement level has 32 loops for hand-guns covering the moat, while the garrison had access to the latter through a sally-port beneath the drawbridge.

Above the basement gallery were a further three tiers of gun positions: within the outer bastions, firing through gun-ports; on the timber platforms of the bastions; and on the roof of the central keep. These two upper tiers of guns fired through embrasures in the parapets. As first constructed, each bastion was hollow and had three gun-ports and four embrasures. The exception was the gatehouse bastion where the gateway replaced the central gun-port. In the parapet of the curtain wall between each bastion was a further embrasure while the keep originally probably had up to eight embrasures. In all, there may have been 39 openings for heavy weapons.

The names of the designers of Henry's fortifications are largely unknown. Only one name can be linked with the great programme of 1539–42 and he was Stephen von Haschenperg, a Moravian. His contribution was limited to Camber Castle near Rye, Sandgate near Folkestone and the earthwork defences linking Walmer, Deal and Sandown. Henry's fortifications owe their design, their distinctive 'house style', to the monarch's own works' organisation responsible for the king's extensive palace building and modernisation programme. Senior officials sent down to supervise construction works at Walmer, Deal and Sandown in the spring of 1539 all came from overseeing building work at the palaces of Nonsuch and Hampton Court. There is also ample evidence that Henry himself took a close personal interest and probably played no small part in the evolution of the fortifications.

The design of the new fortresses stemmed from the circular gun-towers then favoured in northern France and England. The majority of these had been built to defend harbour entrances from attack by hostile warships. Dartmouth, Portsmouth, Camber, Dover and

Cross-section of Walmer Castle in 1741

Hartlepool all had such towers. Mont-St-Michel and St-Malo, ports well known to the English, included round artillery towers in their defences and Henry himself had incorporated such structures into his new defences at Tournai. Castles of the 1539–42 programme were a logical extension, the semi-circular bastions symmetrically arranged around the central tower allowing for the mounting of further tiers of heavy guns.

Although the design of these fortifications was to be superseded in England from the late 1540s by the adoption of angle bastions, they were, when built, a sensible response to immediate needs. In 1539, faced with invasion, Henry and his advisers needed to make likely harbours and anchorages untenable. Raised bastions and gun-towers allowed gunners the advantage of height when firing at warships, while the

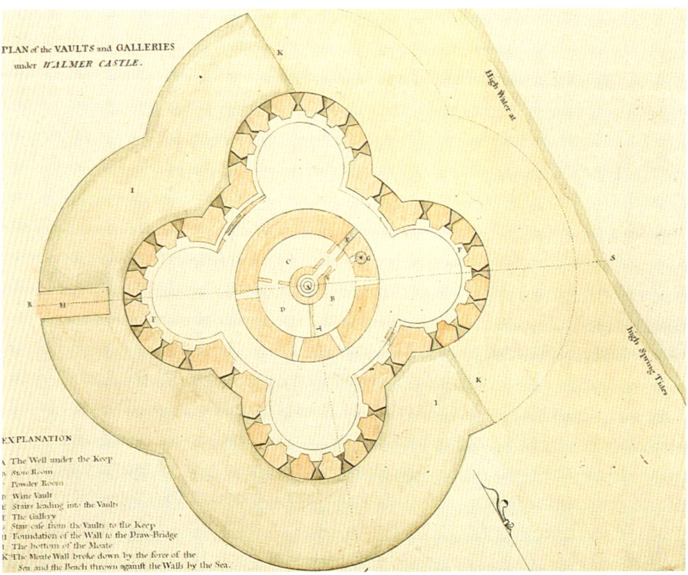

LEFT *Plan of the castle in 1741. The beach was then much closer to the castle's walls*

secondary armament was considered adequate to beat off any landing parties. Warships' armament was not then powerful enough to have made much of an impact on solidly constructed masonry forts. Although Henry's castles would have been vulnerable to prolonged siege with heavy weapons, such an eventuality was probably considered unlikely. In 1588 the Spanish Armada became the first major invasion fleet to sail with a proper siege train of heavy artillery. Significantly, Georgian military engineers faced with a French invasion during the Napoleonic Wars at the beginning of the nineteenth century, came up with a similar solution of strong circular gun-towers – the Martello chain – to beat off warships.

Walmer Castle in the Tudor period

By the beginning of October 1540 Walmer Castle had its first garrison. Under the charge of a captain and his lieutenant were two porters, ten gunners and four soldiers. By then, the threat of invasion had largely passed so these numbers represent the trained nucleus to which additional troops would have been added in the event of actual hostilities. This small garrison was quartered in the central tower, the officers enjoying spacious quarters above the men.

Although we know about the first garrison, we know nothing about the original armament. For local defence against raiding parties, the garrison would have used arquebuses, fired either through the ports covering the moat or over the parapets. These would have been supplemented with bows and arrows. The main armament, capable of engaging warships, could have been a mixture of weapons. Tudor guns, cast from brass and iron, were of many types, patterns and sizes. They ranged from the cannon with its eight-inch calibre and 60lb shot to the small falconet of two-inch calibre firing a pound shot. The extreme range for the larger weapons was about 2000 yards, but their effective range was considerably less.

In 1597 we know that there was one cannon, one culverin, five demi-culverins, a saker, a minion and a falcon at the castle. With the exception of the cannon and the culverin, these were all fairly small weapons. However, in their method of operation they differed little from the eighteenth-century 32-pounders now mounted here.

Like most defence works, Walmer and its neighbours rarely saw any action. The earth bulwarks were soon abandoned, but the castles continued to be garrisoned, if not always kept in good repair. The Downs was too important an anchorage – the only sheltered roadstead between the Thames

A battery of 32-pounder guns on garrison carriages on the east bastion

The castle's rounded bastions and central keep are typical of Henrician fortresses (Aerofilms)

estuary and the Solent – for the defences to be wholly neglected. During the anxious summer of 1588 when the Armada was daily expected, the castles in the Downs were brought to a state of readiness, but thereafter their garrisons had little to do except fire the occasional shot across the bows of foreign ships which had not dipped their flags in salute.

English Civil War

During the English Civil War (1640–51), all three castles were in the hands of Parliamentary forces. However, in the Kentish uprising, which followed the execution of Charles I in 1648, the fleet at the Down came out in favour of the Kentish rebels, as did Sandown Castle. Deal and Walmer joined them shortly afterwards. The uprising was quickly suppressed but the three castles, aided by provisions from the fleet, withstood an army of some 2000 foot soldiers and a few horse under Colonel Rich. These first besieged Walmer, but lacked the heavy artillery essential to force the issue. The castle held out for over three weeks, but lack of any relieving force and probably a shortage of provisions finally caused the garrison to surrender. Colonel Rich, his force now augmented with two cannon and two demi-cannon, then turned his attention to Deal castle, but even with these siege weapons was unable to obtain its surrender for a further three weeks. The castle sustained considerable damage. Sandown surrendered shortly afterwards.

After these stirring events all three castles were repaired. In a letter to the Speaker of the House of Commons, Rich wrote of Walmer '. . . three hundred pounds will complete it. I fear five hundred pounds will scarce render this in so good a condition as it was before it was besieged'.

During the Dutch Wars of the 1650s and 1660s, the three castles proved invaluable in protecting shipping in the Downs, perhaps most notably in the first of the wars. Then, in one incident the Dutch fleet under Van Tromp was unable to capture harried vessels and their ten escorts commanded by Sir George Ayscue which had sought shelter under the guard of the castles' guns.

By the end of the seventeenth century, all three castles became increasingly obsolete as fortresses. Celia Fiennes on her journey through Kent in 1697, referred to them as 'three little forts or castles . . . which hold a few guns but I should think they would be of little effect and give the enemy no great trouble'. By then, Walmer was about to find a new role as the official home of the Lord Warden of the Cinque Ports. Its days as a castle were over; its time as a country residence was about to begin.

The first Lord Warden to live at Walmer was Lionel Sackville, first Duke of Dorset

Residence of the Lords Warden of the Cinque Ports

The Cinque Ports Confederation originated in the eleventh century when the original five port towns – Hastings, Romney, Hythe, Dover and Sandwich – banded together to provide ships and men for the defence of the coast and protection of cross-channel trade. In return for these services they received substantial local privileges including immunity from all external courts of justice and from national taxation. These privileges far outweighed the duties of association, particularly when the latter could serve as cover for little more than licensed piracy. The rapid growth of the confederation and its lack of control became an increasing worry to successive kings.

In the thirteenth century the office of Warden was instituted to oversee and regulate the affairs of the Confederation and to form a direct link with the king and central government. The monarchy further strengthened its control later in the thirteenth century when the post of Warden was combined with that of Constable of Dover Castle. From the fourteenth century, the holder was appointed for life, but the appointment remained firmly in the hands of the king who never allowed it to become hereditary.

By the sixteenth century the importance of the Cinque Ports Confederation was in

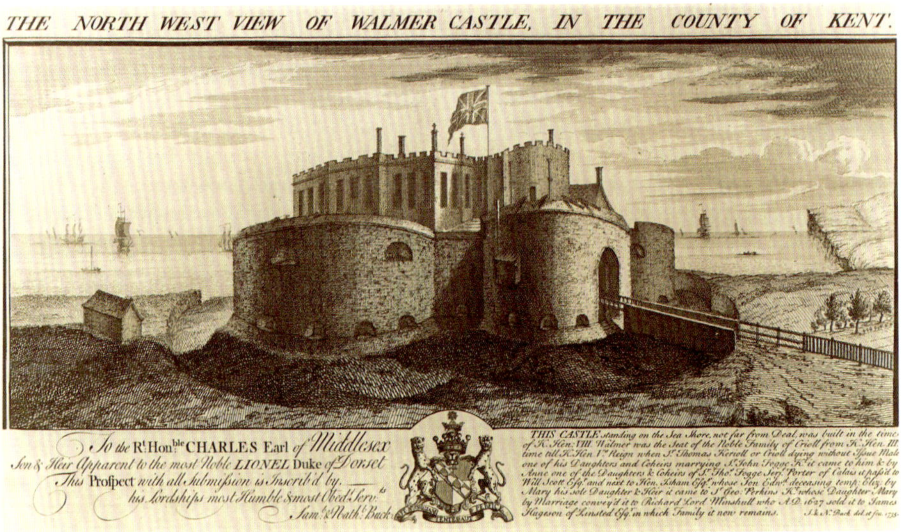

Walmer Castle in 1735. The Tudor gatehouse as it was before it was heightened 150 years later

a decline from which it never recovered. The ports were losing out to changing patterns of foreign trade, while the silting of some harbours prevented their use by larger ships. Furthermore, their importance as providers of fighting ships and troop transports for the Crown disappeared as Tudor monarchs established the Royal Navy on a permanent basis and warships grew in size and evolved their own distinctive design.

Although the disappearance of ship service marked the end of its purpose, the Confederation clung to its privileges, especially judicial freedom, until further reforms in the nineteenth century abolished most of these. A historian of the Cinque Ports wrote, 'The later constitutional history of the Ports is the history of an interesting survival, and of the development of an elaborate system of government for the purpose of maintaining the obsolete privileges of an otherwise purposeless association'.

In the heyday of the Confederation, the office of Lord Warden carried both power and responsibility, as well as considerable scope for personal enrichment. By the nineteenth century the Lord's Warden's power was analogous to that of a Lord Lieutenant and until 1828 he enjoyed a substantial annual salary of £3,000. Throughout its long history, the office has been held by many distinguished people, perhaps no more so than in the last two centuries when it has been increasingly seen as a high honour to be conferred on those who have given especially distinguished service to the State.

In 1708 the Duke of Dorset became the first Lord Warden to use Walmer Castle as his official residence. The compact layout of this obsolete fortress was readily adaptable and the Duke (Lord Warden 1708–13, 1714 and 1728–65) was the first of several tenants to alter and extend the castle to provide accommodation appropriate to their needs. He increased the number of first-floor rooms by building out from the keep over the bastions, as can he seen in the Buck print (above). In the early 1730s a two-storey weather-boarded

One of a number of designs prepared by George Devey for heightening the gatehouse bastion in 1874

The gatehouse bastion today, showing the form of George Devey's final work

The south bastion with its Tudor gun-ports. Since the nineteenth century the moat has been grassed over and planted with flower-beds. The impenetrable thickness of the walls can be judged from the large embrasure (right of centre), which has been modified additionally to provide windows for the ground and first-floor apartments. The doorway is also an addition, built in one of the original Tudor gun-ports, from which a wooden bridge now springs across the moat giving access to the gardens

house was built in the rear of the south bastion as a lodging for the castle gunners; this can still be seen, partly encased by later additions.

The most substantial additions were made by the second Earl Granville (Lord Warden 1865–91). In the year he was appointed, he had married for the second time and he and his young bride set about transforming castle and grounds into a family home. In 1874 they commissioned the architect George Devey to build extra rooms over the gatehouse bastion using stone from Sandown Castle which was then being demolished. One of his architectural drawings of the gatehouse is shown on page 13. Devey's careful additions – he was well-known for his sensitive work on country houses and their gardens – were the last major extensions to the castle.

Gardens

The gardens and grounds surrounding the castle owe much to the enthusiasm of two Lords Warden – William Pitt the Younger (Lord Warden 1792–1806) and the second Earl Granville, some sixty years later. George III had appointed William Pitt as Lord Warden to boost the Prime Minister's small official salary and to ease Pitt's insecure finances. Pitt was delighted with Walmer and visited it as often as his official duties allowed. He was keenly interested in landscape and garden design, and leased extra land at Walmer to the north and west of the castle. In 1803 his niece Lady Hester Stanhope came to live at the castle. In the three years until her uncle's death she immersed herself in improving the grounds. On one occasion she borrowed the local militia for some landscaping and planting intended as a surprise when Pitt returned from London. By the time of his death in 1806 the castle grounds had acquired many features, still

William Pitt, in the uniform of Captain of the Cinque Ports Fencibles, a voluntary force raised during the French Wars. Pitt initiated the landscaping of the grounds

recognisable, including probably the Oval Lawn and the Paddock and the beginnings of the tree shelter belts and plantations.

Despite the indifference and neglect of the three intervening Lords Warden, the Granvilles some sixty years later were able to reinstate much of Pitt and Lady Hester's work. They also added improvements of their own, perhaps most notably the double line of yew hedges and herbaceous borders flanking the gravel walk west of the castle.

The last of the Lords Warden to make any significant additions to the grounds was Lord Beauchamp. Married to Lady Lettice Grosvenor, sister of the Duke of Westminster, the family were leading lights in fashionable London society and during Beauchamp's long Wardenship (1913–34) Walmer was much used for entertainment. Tennis courts were laid out in the walled garden and croquet was played on the lawn.

Later Lords Warden

Most Lords Warden were content to use Walmer Castle and its grounds without making any significant alterations or additions to either. One of the most famous, the Duke of Wellington, was delighted with his castle by the sea. Appointed Lord Warden in January 1829, he stayed here whenever he could, enjoying seabathing, and the company of local friends and their children. In 1835 he was visited here by the sixteen-year-old Princess Victoria, the future queen; seven years later he lent the castle to the Queen and Prince Albert who stayed there with their children for nearly a month in the late autumn of 1842.

The Duke of Wellington lived simply, sleeping on his army camp-bed in his little room overlooking the ramparts and the sea beyond. Here he died in September 1852. His room remains little changed to this day.

The survival of so many furnishings belonging to Lords Warden, such as Wellington and Pitt, is due almost entirely to the initiative of one of their successors, W H Smith, founder of the well-known bookshops, appointed Lord Warden in 1891. Until then, incoming Lords Warden

The extent of the gardens can be seen in this aerial photograph of the castle, looking inshore from the beach

The gardens in 1919. An historic photograph showing the Yew Walk and gardens from the castle (Country Life)

had had to purchase the castle furniture from the family of their predecessors; not all had been willing to do so and furniture with historical associations with the castle was in danger of being lost. W H Smith strove to set up a trust to safeguard such furniture and mementoes, and to ensure that they remained at the castle in perpetuity. Already a sick man when appointed Lord Warden, he died within six months and it was left to his son to create the trust in fulfilment of his father's wishes. A fuller account of the arrangements is given on page 33. The Heirloom furniture as it is known, is distinguished by small numbered brass plates. Later Lords Warden have added to the collection.

In recent years, Lords Warden have been provided with private apartments above the gatehouse. Sir Winston Churchill (Lord Warden 1941–65) never stayed here, but his successor Sir Robert Menzies, Prime Minister of Australia, was an enthusiastic visitor. The present Lord Warden, Her Majesty Queen Elizabeth the Queen Mother, makes regular use of the castle and is keenly interested in it and the grounds. A new garden was designed for the Queen Mother by Penelope Hobhouse in 1997, to mark her ninety-fifth birthday. Walmer thus remains very much a castle with a purpose. None of Henry VIII's fortresses has had a more active history, first as one of 'the castles which keep the Downs', then continuing the link as residence of the Lord Warden, one of whose main tasks was once the defence of these narrow seas.

The Duke of Wellington, a popular hero after the defeat of Napolean at Waterloo, is seen here in the uniform of Field Marshal

William Henry Smith was instrumental in preserving the Heirloom furniture and other mementoes at Walmer

Earl Granville, who did much to modernise the castle's residential accommodation and develop the surrounding gardens

Lords Warden since 1708

Duke of Dorset (1708)
Duke of Ormonde (1713)
Duke of Dorset (1714)
Earl of Leicester (1717)
Duke of Dorset (1728)
Earl of Holderness (1765)
Earl of Guilford (1778)
Rt Hon William Pitt (1792)
Earl of Liverpool (1806)
Duke of Wellington (1829)
Marquess of Dalhousie (1853)
Viscount Palmerston (1861)
Earl Granville (1865)

Marquess Curzon of Kedleston, seen here as the Viceroy of India 1899–1905, became an enthusiastic historian of Walmer

Earl Beauchamp, who made much use of the castle as a weekend country-house and holiday home for his large family

Rt Hon W H Smith (1891)
Marquess of Dufferin and Ava (1891)
Marquess of Salisbury (1895)
Marquess Curzon of Kedleston (1904)
HRH Prince of Wales (1905)
Earl Brassey (1907)
Earl Beauchamp (1913)
Marquess of Reading (1934)
Marquess of Willingdon (1936)
Sir Winston Churchill (1941)
Sir Robert Menzies (1965)
HM Queen Elizabeth the Queen Mother (1978)

Winston Churchill, acknowledging the crowds at his installation. Like Wellington, he was an immensely popular wartime hero

Lord and Lady Beauchamp on 18 July 1914 at the installation ceremony of the office of Lord Warden of the Cinque Ports. The historic pageantry attracted a large number of visitors to Dover, where the streets were 'gaily decorated' and lined with troops. Military bands played at various points along the processional route. Lord Beauchamp was accompanied by 'gorgeously clad' Coronation Barons in scarlet cloaks trimmed with blue and gold. A fleet of warships in the harbour were dressed 'rainbow fashion'. (Photo: London News Agency)

Rooms and their Contents

Presentation of the Rooms

Over the centuries the interiors of Walmer Castle were constantly changed, not only in decoration but also in function and structure. Each successive Lord Warden adapted the rooms to suit his requirements. As a result the interiors have evolved by a process of modification.

To try to return them to their appearance during the time of any one Lord Warden – the Duke of Wellington, for instance – would involve the removal of additions and changes made by his successors. Nor is there sufficient evidence in the form of inventories or original fragments of carpets and textiles to re-create the earlier periods.

The castle is shown in its 1930s form, when it was last used as a residence. This period is well documented, including photographs, enabling the interiors to be recreated faithfully.

Of the last three resident occupants, Lords Reading and Willingdon stored much of the historic furniture, preferring to use their own pieces; their immediate predecessor, the Earl Beauchamp, who made great use of the castle as a weekend country-house and holiday home for his large family, used many of the historic furnishings. The arrangement of the Dining, Drawing and Ante Rooms as well as the Corridor conform closely to those during the Beauchamp family occupancy.

Reactions to Walmer as a residence varied widely. Some Lords Warden, such as the Marquess of Dufferin and Ava, were absentee Wardens; others, such as Lord Salisbury, seemed relatively disinterested,

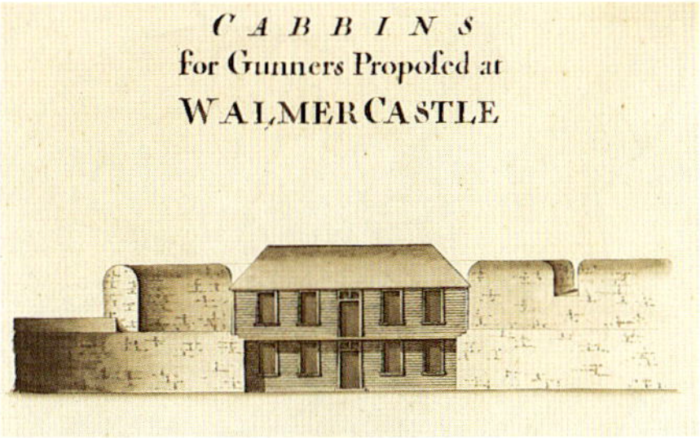

The Gunners' Lodging of c1730, from a drawing dated 1741

while Lord Curzon at one stage described the castle as unfit for human habitation (though undoubtedly this negative reaction was largely influenced by his wife's serious illness, ascribed to the castle's poor sanitation). The more typical reaction was that of the Duke of Wellington who described Walmer as 'his charming marine residence', an opinion shared by many of its occupants, their families and friends.

Until the early years of this century, Walmer Castle remained the responsibility of the War Office; by 1905 when it no longer had a military function, it was transferred to the Ministry of Works and shortly after was opened to the public. It is now looked after by English Heritage.

Gunners' Lodging

The Gunners' Lodging, a two-storeyed weather-boarded structure, was one of the earliest additions to the fabric of the castle, making it more suitable for domestic use. It comprises two rooms on both ground and first floors each side of a central corridor and was built around 1730, during the Duke of Dorset's tenure. As the name indicates, the ground-floor area provided

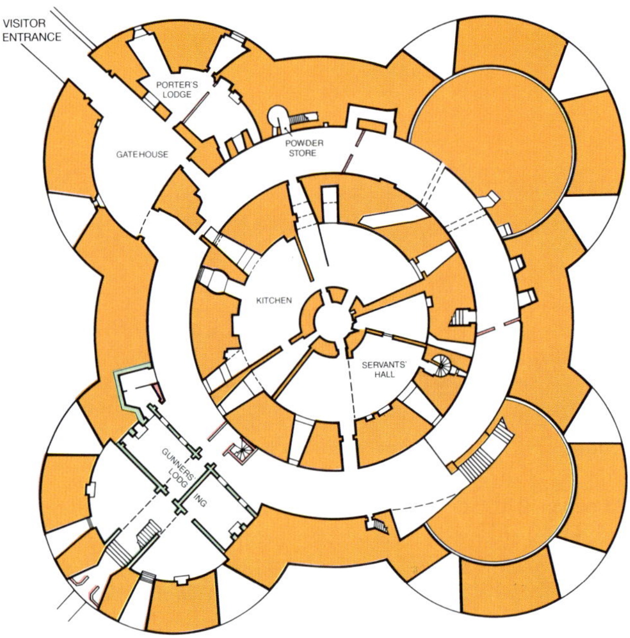

Ground floor

In this plan of the ground floor the original Tudor gun embrasures in the bastions are clearly visible

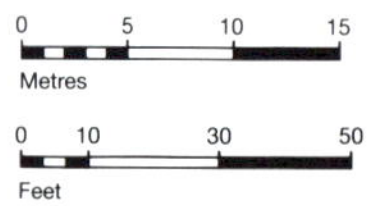

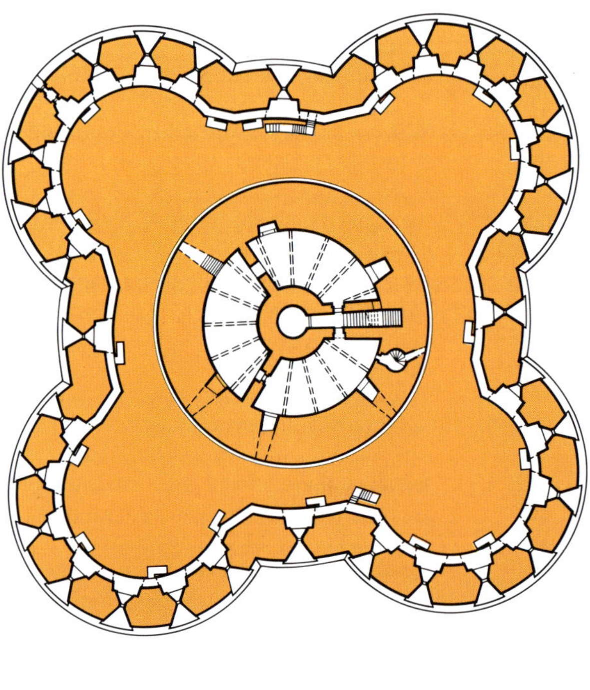

Basement

The basement of the keep contained the well, and was used for stores and munitions. The firing loops in the bastion walls covered the moat and were designed for handguns

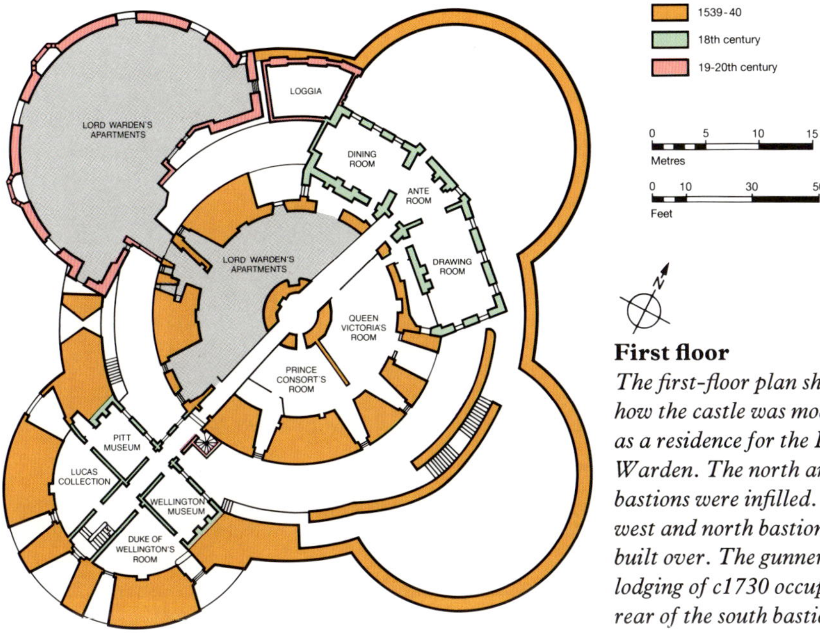

First floor

The first-floor plan shows how the castle was modified as a residence for the Lords Warden. The north and east bastions were infilled. The west and north bastions were built over. The gunners' lodging of c1730 occupied the rear of the south bastion

accommodation for the gunners, while the upper rooms were reserved for the use of officers. Use of the castle as a residence by the 1740s is confirmed by the survival of several inventories detailing lists of beds, linen and plate.

Over the centuries the ground-floor rooms changed from being adjoining dressing-rooms to a guest bedroom created by Pitt, and then to part of the service area of the castle, housing the butlers of successive Lords Warden. In 1939 the partitions between the rooms were removed by Lady Willingdon, wife of the last resident Lord Warden, opening up most of the ground floor for circulation during parties and other entertainments. At this time, the room became the entrance hall to the house and contained a mixture of country furniture of differing periods. The large print, *His Last Return from Duty*, after James Glass, shows Wellington leaving Horse Guards for the last time as Commander-in-Chief.

East and West Lounges

These two rooms were built in the space between the Gunners' Lodging and the bastion wall a decade or so later than the Gunners' Lodging and were recorded as being complete by 1746; they were used as extra bedrooms for visitors during William Pitt's time. Lady Granville used the West Lounge as a dressing room, with a large window inserted into the casemate by George Devey giving a view on to the kitchen garden. By the 1930s when the Beauchamp family was in residence for long periods in the summer, the East Lounge was used as a bedroom for four housemaids.

The West Lounge houses a number of items which are associated with William Pitt. The set of six leather-seated mahogany dining-chairs certainly belonged to him and are marked with brass

The Lucas Room, which houses an extensive collection of Wellington memorabilia

plates. The plates were added by Lord and Lady Granville who had intended them to be less conspicuous, but they were fixed in their absence. The mahogany desk corresponds very closely with the description of one noted in the Walmer account books for 26 June 1798 ('a mahogany library table with drawers on one side and panell door with pidgionhole on other side covered with green cloath and on large casters') costing eighteen pounds and eight shillings. The rococo-style mahogany framed armchairs in the East Lounge were also possibly part of the furnishings in Pitt's time.

Staircase and Landing

On the window sill stands a bust of the Duke of Wellington by the Italian sculptor Peter Turnerelli, which was first loaned to Walmer Castle from the Royal Collection by King Edward VII in 1904. It formed part of the contents of George IV's demolished Carlton House, where it was displayed as part of decorations of the fête held in 1814 to celebrate the Duke of Wellington's victories.

Lucas Room

This room with its modern wallpaper of mid nineteenth-century design, replica moreen curtains and loop-pile Brussels-weave carpet provides an appropriate setting for the Lucas Collection of Wellington *memorabilia*. This collection was assembled by Wing-Commander Thomas Hill Lucas (1895–1975) with great discernment and donated by him in 1966 to the Ministry of Works. The variety of objects and works of art illustrate the great and enduring popularity of the 'Iron Duke' – Arthur Wellesley, First Duke of Wellington. Wellington's military reputation reached its peak between 1810

A selection of items depicting Wellington in the Lucas Collection

and 1815, culminating in the Battle of Waterloo and the final defeat of Napoleon.

As his fame spread throughout Europe, his portrait was in great demand by the hero-worshipping public. After his military career ended, Wellington went into politics and remained in the public eye through the work of engravers and caricaturists. Besides engravings and a fine range of portrait busts of varying scales and media, there are also humbler objects – transfer-printed pot lids, paperweights and doorstops, all stamped with his unmistakable likeness.

The two wall cabinets contain a fine and varied collection of coins, which are cast in a variety of metals and celebrate different aspects of Wellington's life.

Duke of Wellington's Room

It was in this room, seated in the armchair with its yellow striped chintz cover, that Wellington died at 3.25pm on 14 September 1852.

He had been Lord Warden for 23 years, spending much time at Walmer. His body lay in state in this room, the walls draped with black, for two months before the state funeral in St Paul's Cathedral. On the final two days before his remains were taken to London, between eight and nine thousand local people came to pay their respects.

All other rooms in the castle have radically altered in form and decoration, but this room still bears the character of the Duke, being practical, even spartan in its furnishings. After Wellington's death the room was used for differing purposes. Before George Devey's additions provided extra accommodation for the Granvilles, it served as a nursery for their children.

Traditionally, a new Lord Warden bought the furniture and contents of the castle from his predecessor's estate, but Lord Palmerston at first declined to do this. To prevent Wellington's possessions being dispersed, the second Duke removed items to Apsley House for safekeeping. After W H Smith initiated the Indenture of Heirlooms by Act of Parliament to ensure the retention of historic items, these pieces were returned to Walmer.

Alterations continued to be made – Lady Salisbury removed the original bookshelves and substituted glazed doors, an act much criticized by Lord Curzon. The present appearance of the room, however, is due to the pioneering work of Lady Reading. During her husband's brief tenure (1934–35), she took a great interest in the history of Walmer and its occupants and attempted to recreate the room as it had been at Wellington's death, drawing on descriptions and surviving fragments. Having found a sample of wallpaper in the castle which she thought to be of Wellington's time, Lady Reading had it copied (the pattern does not correspond entirely with that seen in watercolours of the Duke's room and Lady Reading may well have copied a piece of paper supplied in the 1890s for Lady Salisbury by Herbert J Clarabut, 'General Draper and Complete House Furnishers' of Deal.

The original carpet did not survive, but instead a faded fragmentary example from Apsley House (and also seen in a portrait of the Duke in his study at Stratfield Saye) was used as a model. The brass-framed campaign-bed with its canvas base and leather webbing retains all its original bedding – a horsehair mattress covered with silk, a bolster in a chamois leather cover, silk headboard, a bound blanket and a quilt of 'blueish-green shot silk'.

Here at Walmer (as at Apsley House, his London home, and his country house of Stratfield Saye) yellow seems to have been the predominant colour and is recorded as having been used for curtains and squab cushions in several other rooms, as well as the curtains, chintz chair cover and carpet

in this room at Walmer.

The prints hanging in the room correspond almost exactly with those in Wellington's day, as can be seen in the watercolours of the 1840s, copies after Thomas Shotter Boys. Above the

The Duke of Wellington's Room, which is arranged as it was when he was Lord Warden from 1829 to 1852. The room closely matches a contemporary watercolour painting by Thomas Shotter Boys. The simple furnishings bear witness to the character of the 'Iron Duke' who preferred unsophisticated surroundings. In the room are his campaign-bed on which he slept, and the armchair in which he died in 1852

Wellington's campaign-bed, which still retains its original horsehair mattress and bedding

chimney-piece is a print of Prince Arthur, Queen Victoria and Prince Albert's third son and Wellington's godson. The curtains are carefully produced replicas of the originals, which survived in shattered state, and are made of yellow moreen lined with red tammy.

Wellington Museum

The collection in the Museum is also due to Lady Reading, who gathered together items associated with the Duke's long tenancy. These included many personal possessions and *memorabilia*, among them a pair of famous 'Wellington boots' and a pair of overboots, Wellington's uniform jackets as Field Marshal and as Lord Warden. In contrast to the commemorative items on display in the Lucas Room, these exhibits highlight the private side of Wellington's life.

The Museum was originally situated in the Gunners' Lodging below, but was moved to its current position by Lady Willingdon. During Wellington's lifetime, this room was a bedroom, used by his Parliamentary colleague and great friend, Arbuthnot. The large print of *Chelsea Pensioners reading the Waterloo Dispatch* is after Sir David Wilkie's painting at Apsley House. The marquetry picture over the chimney-piece also belonged to Wellington. Made by the estate carpenter, it depicts his country house, Stratfield Saye. It was a favourite piece of the Duke's and during his lifetime hung in the Dining Room recess.

Pitt Museum

William Pitt's own study and bedroom

The creation of the Wellington Museum reflected the interest shown by successive Lords Warden in preserving the personal effects of Wellington

Wellington's famous boots

Wellington's jacket as Lord Warden

form part of the present Lord Warden's private apartment and cannot be viewed, but this small room contains a few of the items associated with Pitt, notably part of the set of satinwood armchairs and the leather-covered library or gaming chair. On the floor is an ingrain carpet woven after a nineteenth-century pattern, as are the dimity curtains. Both are types of furnishing recorded as having been used by Pitt at Walmer and Holmwood, his country house which he was forced to give up in 1803 for financial reasons, when he moved permanently to Walmer. The display cabinet contains a few items associated with Pitt and his father, Pitt the Elder, Earl of Chatham, given by his niece, Miss Madeleine Pitt-Taylor and by Lord Curzon. The walls are hung with a selection of prints and mezzotints of Pitt,

This library or gaming chair is among a number of items belonging to William Pitt which are exhibited at Walmer

The Pitt Museum, although not the room he occupied,

as well as several contemporary caricatures given by Lord Reading.

Corridor

The collection of prints in the Corridor is an example of the many influences on the interiors at Walmer; those in heavy gilt

ontains many historic items associated with Pitt, as well as prints and portraits

frames in the Lantern were in the Drawing Room in Wellington's time, but had been moved to their current position by the 1890s.

In the section of the Corridor between the Wellington and Pitt Museums, there hang three framed Heirloom lists and a fine mezzotint of W H Smith, to whom survival of so many of the Heirloom items is due. Smith, a member of the publishing family and a prominent Conservative politician, was appointed Lord Warden in 1891, but already ill at the time, died some six months later. In that short time, he nevertheless took a great interest in Walmer's history and was particularly

In Tudor times the Lantern was the central stairwell of the keep. Prints hung in the Lantern and Corridor represent the range of interests of successive Lords Warden

concerned with preventing the removal of items with historical associations (as nearly happened in the case of some of Wellington's possessions). Traditionally each Lord Warden bought the contents at a given valuation, with a sum deducted for wear and tear. The items then became the Lord Warden's personal property. Smith proposed to establish items with historical associations as Heirlooms, which could not be removed from Walmer and, though at the disposal of Lord Warden, had to be maintained in good condition. He formulated an Act of Parliament detailing the conditions and listing the items (stipulating that the framed list was to be hung in the Corridor); there was also provision for additions to the Heirlooms by subsequent Lords Warden.

W H Smith died before he was able to implement his intentions and it was left to his son W F D Smith, with the agreement of the Marquess of Dufferin and Ava, Smith's successor as Lord Warden, to complete the formalities. Lady Granville, the wife of Smith's predecessor, had always been very interested in the history of Walmer and in 1892 was allowed by Lord Dufferin to attach small brass numbered plates to identify the Heirloom items; many of these can still be seen today.

The Granvilles painted the Corridor a 'soft Morris blueish green' (previously it was grained in imitation oak, as in the three reception rooms). This colour was maintained by their successors with little variation and has been restored after microscopic analysis of paint cross-sections.

In the section of Corridor by the windows is a series of plans and elevations collected and given by Lord Curzon, which illustrate the many phases of building at Walmer. The top-lit central section, known as the Lantern, was created by George Devey for the Granvilles and is hung with prints of Wellington, George IV and other monarchs. Further along the Corridor on the left, hang photographs of the twentieth-century Lords Warden. Other prints of artists and genre scenes are typical of those collected and displayed, particularly by Earl Beauchamp.

Queen Victoria's and the Prince Consort's Rooms

These are two of the rooms occupied by the royal couple during their month-long visit to Walmer in 1842 with their two eldest children. For the visit, the partition wall between Pitt's study and bedroom in the Lord Warden's apartment was demolished to create a private dining room, furniture was brought in specially, and the Duke of Wellington moved out, staying in the Ship Hotel at Dover. Very little of the furniture from the visit survives – the armchair and *chaise-longue*, and the four-post bed, which was moved and cut down by later Lords Warden (Lady Granville confessed this in a letter to Lord Curzon: 'We were Goths enough to cut it down to a half tester, but must plead as excuse that it was a hideous object with curtains and deep valence and canopy, all in yellow moreen with a woollen fringe'). The present chintz hangings, much faded, date from around 1900 when Lady Salisbury returned the bed to the room and refurbished it.

The prints of Queen Victoria and the Prince Consort were given as Heirlooms by Lord Salisbury, though Lady Granville notes that they were given to her husband by Queen Victoria on a visit to Balmoral Castle. The armchair and *chaise-longue* are covered in a copy of a chintz, which was found by Lady Beauchamp and described by her husband as 'a delightful old chintz for the furniture connected with Queen Victoria which shows her profile and that of the Prince Consort

Queen Victoria's room in 1919. The existing partition was reinstated in 1994 (Country Life)

among little bunches of flowers'.

The Prince Consort's Room, which Wellington used as his library, was also emptied for the Royal visit to provide two adjoining rooms, each with a small dressing room. Throughout the nineteenth and twentieth centuries these two rooms were used as the principal bedrooms of the Lords Warden, until the evacuation in 1939 at the outset of the Second World War.

Ante Room, Dining Room and Drawing Room

The Ante Room and the adjoining Dining and Drawing Rooms were built in the 1740s, probably as four small rooms, but by 1785 a visitor credits Pitt with having removed a partition to create a large drawing room. All three rooms have panes of tinted glass which are thought to have been put in by Lord Liverpool, for the comfort of his wife whose eyes were troubled by strong light.

The Ante Room contains part of a set of fine views of the castle, as well as Dover and Deal of the 1730s.

The Dining Room contains a set of thirteen mahogany chairs which belonged to William Pitt; originally they were cane-seated with squab cushions, but in the 1860s Lady Granville had them upholstered in the existing red morocco for use as dining chairs. The large collection of prints was assembled by Lord Granville, and provides portraits of most of the holders of the office of Lord Warden from the earliest time. They are hung as they were in the nineteenth century, with the earliest to the left of the chimney-piece; in the piers between the windows are prints and photographs of the nineteenth-century Lords Warden.

The Drawing Room is displayed as it

The Dining Room is hung with portraits of the holders of the office of Lord Warden

looked in the 1920s and 1930s (see photograph on page 40) when the castle was last used as a residence by Lord Beauchamp, who spent extended summer holidays there with his large family. That it was still a family home is attested to by the frequent references in the accounts to repairs to furniture. The furniture includes a fine set of late eighteenth-century painted beechwood furniture, comprising sofa, armchairs, and window seats. The two anonymous seventeenth-century oil paintings show different views of Dover Castle.

A Tour of the Grounds

Plan of the grounds of Walmer Castle

There is no formal route around the gardens. Visit whichever parts you like, using the map, or stroll from one area to another.

The Broad Walk (1)

Here a double herbaceous border provides a riot of summer colour, with groups of bearded irises, lilies and alliums.

The yew hedges were once a neat and narrow backdrop to the borders. During the last fifty years, old age and snow damage have allowed them to develop into the huge rolling hedges, full of picturesque humps and bumps, for which Walmer is known.

The Terraces (2)

The terraces were designed by William Masters in 1866 to form a transition

The Broad Walk gardens in the summer; a double herbaceous border provides a riot of colour

between the formality of the Broad Walk to the paddock beyond. The lower terrace was enlarged to form a rectangular lawn by Lady Beauchamp in the 1920s and Lady Willingdon used it as a croquet lawn in the late 1930s. Today the lower terrace is once again being used for croquet and the upper area contains colourful annual bedding, incorporating the rose 'Queen Mother'.

The lower terrace, which is now used as a croquet lawn

The Paddock (3) via the Woodland Walk (10)

This informal garden contains a variety of ornamental trees, including flowering cherries and birch. Daffodils abound in the spring, followed by a meadow of wild flowers in the early summer, and carpets of pink cyclamen and autumn crocuses under mature evergreen oaks later in the year. Flowering shrubs were first added between the wars. The shelter belts on the perimeter were badly damaged in the storms of the late 1980s and there has been extensive replanting.

The Glen (4)

Beyond the paddock is a chalk quarry. Although not currently open, it can be seen from the paddock. Here, in around 1803, Lady Hester Stanhope made her 'glen', a pattern of steep woodland walks under gloomy trees, in the picturesque

Further Reading

The Drawing Room in 1919, when the Beauchamp family was in residence (Country Life)

COLVIN, H M, *The History of the King's Works*, vol IV, part 2. London, 1982

CONWAY, M, 'Walmer Castle, Kent' *Country Life*, 1919

CURZON, Lord, 'Personal History of Walmer Castle and its Lords Warden' *Country Life*, 1927

ELVIN, R S, *The History of Walmer and Walmer Castle* Canterbury, 1894

JERVIS, S and TOMLIN, M, *Apsley House : Wellington Museum* London, 1990

LUCY, H, 'Lords Warden of the Cinque Ports' *Pall Mall Magazine*, 1895

MAXWELL, H E, *The Life and Times of W H Smith* London, 1893

MURRAY, K M E, *Constitutional History of the Cinque Ports* Manchester, 1935